MACULAR DEGENERATION

A JOURNEY OUT OF SIGHT

By

ROSE GASSER

and

LOIS BROOKS

Disclaimer

While the publisher, editors, authors, and advisors have made every effort to ensure the accuracy of the information in *Macular Degeneration: A Journey Out of Sight*, they assume no responsibility for either typographical or informational errors, inaccuracies, omissions of either people or places, or any other inconsistencies within the book. Any slights of people or organizations are totally unintentional. Any misuse or improper use of written material is totally unintentional.

ISBN 1-4251-1364-8

Trafford 06-3123

Table of Contents

Note for Librarians: A cataloguing record for this book is available from Library and Archives
Canada at www.collectionscanada.ca/amicus/index-e.html
ISBN 1-4251-1364-8

Printed in Victoria, BC, Canada. Printed on paper with minimum 30% recycled fibre.
Trafford's print shop runs on "green energy" from solar, wind and other environmentally-friendly power sources.

TRAFFORD
PUBLISHING™
Offices in Canada, USA, Ireland and UK

Book sales for North America and international:
Trafford Publishing, 6E–2333 Government St.,
Victoria, BC V8T 4P4 CANADA
phone 250 383 6864 (toll-free 1 888 232 4444)
fax 250 383 6804; email to orders@trafford.com
Book sales in Europe:
Trafford Publishing (UK) Limited, 9 Park End Street, 2nd Floor
Oxford, UK OX1 1HH UNITED KINGDOM
phone +44 (0)1865 722 113 (local rate 0845 230 9601)
facsimile +44 (0)1865 722 868; info.uk@trafford.com
Order online at:
trafford.com/06-3123

10 9 8 7 6 5 4 3 2

Acknowledgements

We sincerely appreciate all the support we received from our writer's group in Roseville, California, who encouraged us to complete our book and helped to make it available to all of you who are desperately in need of encouragement.

Thanks to the following: Marion Applegate, Joanne Burkett, Tom Hatcher, Jennifer Martin, Dorothy Maurer, and Ron Retterer.

A special word of appreciation goes to our families for their support, especially Whit Gasser and Nancy Morin.

We are ever so grateful and owe so much to the magnificent staff of the Society for the Blind. Without their patience and training, we would still be stumbling in the dark.

Introduction

Confronted by vision loss due to macular degeneration, two women take you on a journey, which started when they were first diagnosed with this disease.

You will learn how they were informed about losing their sight and their gradual realization that, on this new journey, there was no return trip.

This true story tells of their personal experiences while coping with the disease which turned their lives upside down and what they did to right themselves.

Come along with Rose and Lois as they share their feelings, problems, and solutions during their journey out of sight.

This book was written to help those of you who will take the time and energy to read it. You will discover you are not the only ones who have had to travel along this same bumpy road. And you will find, not only are you in charge of your own destiny, there is a whole new life waiting for you. Those of us who are facing this journey of no return can take heart from the sage words of Patrick Overton:

When we walk to the edge of all the light we have
And take a step into the darkness of the unknown,
We must believe that one of two things will happen.
There will be something solid for us to stand on
Or we will be taught to fly.

Hope sees the invisible, feels the intangible, and achieves the impossible.
—Anonymous

Chapter 1: Hope

We are two women who grew up in different states, California and Iowa. We probably would never have met if we had not run into a bump in the road of life called macular degeneration. This disease has no known cause or cure, as yet, and slowly, but surely, will lead to blindness.

At the time of the onset of macular degeneration, we had each raised our families, retired from successful careers, and were looking forward to enjoying our golden years.

As you can imagine, both of us were completely devastated and, at first, refused to believe macular degeneration could possibly be happening to us. After going through all the stages of denial, anger, bargaining, and depression, we were left with no choice but to accept the fact that this disease had chosen us. No doubt about it. It was the largest boulder on the bumpy road of life we had ever encountered.

We decided to face this challenge as we had faced any problem in life before, and, through our journey out of sight, we discovered we were very much alike. We both were determined, upbeat, and resilient. We have discovered that nothing substantially has really changed for us, except we had to learn to live our lives slightly differently.

The first thing we learned was to accept the fact the macular was not going away, unless some miracle drug was discovered. Yes, we were hopeful someday there would be a cure, but we had no intention of moping around waiting for this to happen. We opted for hoping, not moping.

We have both lived very active lives and would love to do exactly what we want for the rest of our lives. Although our families were very sympathetic and willing to help us, we soon learned we'd better darned well figure out how to do things for our-selves. We had been too independent all of our lives, for one thing. Plus, neither one of us were prone to participate in any pity parties because we believed no healthy human being thrives on self-pity. We didn't want to have family and friends hovering over us, feeling sorry for us, either.

We also didn't play the blame game. Loss of vision just happens and seems to be happening more often all the time. There's no one to blame. Macular degeneration was something we were dealt in the game of life. We decided to learn to deal with it.

One of the main reasons for sharing our story with you is to assure you there is hope! We will be repeating ourselves throughout the book. The reason for doing so is to reinforce our message and show you that you, too, can overcome your feelings of depression and loneliness. We have been there, so we recognize the symptoms. Don't try to hide your feelings behind closed doors. We've been there, too. Open those doors and feel the warmth of the sun shining brightly, telling you today will be a brighter day.

We are convinced our hopeful attitudes permeated all of our decisions and were the reason we were able to overcome fear and doubt.

How did we meet? We had a mutual friend who was aware of our macular degeneration. This friend knew Lois had been attending a support group for the vision impaired and encouraged Rose to contact her. Rose finally attended one of the meetings and, right away, we knew this was the beginning of a beautiful friendship.

With the help and support from the Society for the Blind, we have been given hope. We have learned to laugh again and enjoy our God-given talents. We take joy in just being ourselves and doing the things we know are awaiting us.

We have a desire to reach each of you with our story. We want you to join us on our journey. Maybe we can encourage you to live again, filled with hope for a very bright future.

Life is like an onion; you peel it off one layer at a time, and sometimes you weep.
—Carl Sandburg

Chapter 2: What Is Macular Degeneration?

First, it will be helpful to describe what macular degeneration is in order to help you understand how our sight has been affected. We hope our explanation will help everyone better understand how important the macula is in enabling us to have sight.

As the light enters our eyes, it is focused onto the retina. The light is then converted into sharp central images. The light falling on the sidewalls of the retina is what we will see out of the corners of our eye—the peripheral vision. The macula is the retina's 'bulls eye' where the sharp images are processed and carried to the brain by the optic nerve.

The macula is made up of several layers. The light-sensing cells produce the sharp central vision. The second layer, *pigments epithelium*, nourishes the cells. The third layer, *choroids*, contains blood vessels, which transport nourishment and carry away waste material.

There are actually two types of macular degeneration— the dry type and the wet type—each leading to a sharp loss of vision.

The dry type is a gradual loss of vision because parts of

the macula have begun to die. The vision becomes blurry, leaving blank spots and causing wavy lines. Usually this is a slower process. Those who have the dry type often retain their peripheral vision. However, the dry type can often lead to the wet type of macular degeneration, which may result in a sudden loss of vision.

The wet type is caused when abnormal blood vessels grow for some unknown reason, leaking fluid or blood. The build up of this fluid causes the macula to bulge, distorting our vision. With this wet type, we may see dark spots in the center of our vision due to this fluid under the macula. This wet type often leads to sudden vision loss.

Even though the diagnosis may be macular degeneration, there are also many other causes of vision loss.

Macular degeneration is more common in people over 65 years of age, although it can affect younger ones as well. There are millions of age-related macular degeneration cases in the United States alone. Of these, only ten percent are diagnosed with the wet type, and only twenty percent of these may go totally blind.

There is much research currently being conducted on finding a cure for macular degeneration, but first researchers need to identify its cause. Until then, whether we develop the wet or dry types, we will have to make significant changes in how we choose to live our lives.

Macular Chart

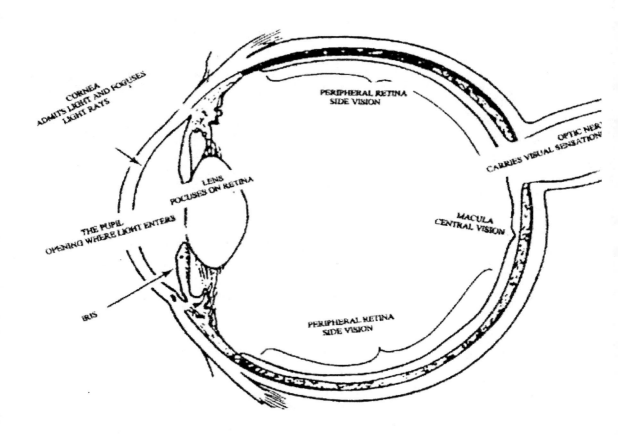

If you're going to walk on thin ice,
you might as well dance.
—Anonymous

Chapter 3: Shades of Blue

Can you imagine waking up every day in a constant fog? That's what we see every morning. We are not able to distinguish colors. What may look brown to Rose may look blue to Lois. When we look out the window, there may be children playing, but we cannot see their faces. Rose may just see their legs and the tops of their heads. Lois may just see a blur. Some people with macular degeneration can still see to drive, even though it isn't always a wise thing to do. Yet, that same person may be unable to read the newspaper or look up numbers in the phone directory.

Our vision loss may be so gradual, we don't realize it is happening. Often we explain it as "old age catching up with me." Ours, Rose and Lois's, has been a slow loss of vision, although there are others who have experienced, for various reasons, a sudden vision loss.

Once, at an intensive retreat, our counselor compared our vision to the shades of blue. With the color blue, no two people see the same shade. At first, this seemed rather puzzling, but soon the pieces of the puzzle fell into place.

The world is full of so many shades of blue, and no two of

them are exactly the same. Looking at the sky or the ocean, how many different shades do we see? There are endless shades of blue, and no two are identical. Our vision is definitely similar to this.

Because we lost our vision gradually, we didn't notice all the changes in our world at once. It started with small things, like how the newspaper print in our morning paper seemed smaller than usual. Or, when we just dropped something on the floor, we couldn't see to find it. Daily chores were becoming more difficult. It's no wonder the first thing we did was run to the eye doctor to get stronger glasses.

Eventually, as we lost more of our vision, we were sent to a specialist. What a shock it was to learn that not only did we have macular degeneration, but there is no cure for it, and eventually we may go blind.

What were we going to do about it? We had two choices. We could sit around moping and feeling sorry for ourselves, or we could consult with another specialist to learn more about the condition. Although the answer was still the same, we refused to give in without trying every avenue.

The doctors suggested several things to try, but made no guarantees. What works for one person may not necessarily work for someone else, they said. Very few, if any, of the doctors told us to search for a support group for help.

Luckily, we experienced the support group for ourselves. What an eye opener it was! We not only supported each other emotionally and spiritually, but we gathered tons of ideas from people who had a wealth of knowledge in all kinds of areas. We soaked up all the information we could, even if it was as simple as which vitamins and herbs might help slow down the deterioration of our vision. We were of the opinion, if it helped someone else, it might just help us as well.

Just because we couldn't see the little kids playing across the street, didn't mean we couldn't stop and listen to their chatter or laughter to picture their activities. We learned to really listen to the cars and buses moving along beside us on the road, and soon we were able to determine in which direction they were going. Were we surprised to discover we would be able to cross the street safely? You bet!

We listened to the breeze blowing through the trees and the birds happily singing, telling us it was a nice day. We felt the moisture on the grass as we walked, so knew it was still early in the morning. The warm sun was on our backs, telling us we were probably walking west. Then we felt the sidewalk under our feet. With the use of our trusted canes, we knew we were walking safely.

By using our sense of feel, we also identified items in the kitchen. We knew when we had spilled something on the counter or when someone else had made a mess in the kitchen.

Just as important and useful to us was our sense of smell. We smelled the soap and shampoo we were using. We sniffed our clean clothes as we dressed. The aroma coming from the kitchen told us what we were having for dinner. When we went shopping, we could always find Starbucks, See's candy store, and the bakery by their wonderful smells.

Using all of our senses seemed to give us a better perspective on how to relate to our new world. It was useless to cling to the way things were. We knew we were just two people out of millions caught in the web of macular degeneration. Even though we had crossed over many bumps in life's road, we were not going to sit around doing nothing. As long as there was so much available out there to help us lead productive lives, we were determined to share our story with you and let you know where we were then and how far we've come now.

**The fool wonders, the wise man asks.
—Benjamin Disraeli**

Chapter 4: Rose's Story

For well over twenty years now, I have been haunted by a conversation I had with a doctor, a memory which, in retrospect, was a warning that should have made me realize I had better do something.

"Mrs. Gasser, may I take a picture of your eyes?"

"Why?" I asked inquisitively.

"I found a spot on the back of your eye, and I want to keep a check on it. It's nothing to worry about, but, the next time you come into the office, we can check to see if there's been any change."

You're probably wondering, *Why didn't the stupid girl go back?*

Well, I did. I went back to the optometrist who said there was very little change in my sight. He said there was no need to change the lenses, but I did anyway because I wanted newer, more stylish frames.

A couple of years later I returned to have my eyes examined. The doctor had acquired a large practice by then and was in the process of opening another office.

Unable to see my original optometrist, I settled for seeing his assistant. I asked if he could see the spot in my eye, but he told me everything was fine. He looked for my records but could not find them.

Years went by. I went to a different doctor. Of course, my lenses were stronger with each new pair of glasses I purchased. Other than stronger lenses, nothing more was ever mentioned about the spot. That is, until the year 2003.

I'd been a real estate broker for twenty-seven years and had a great job with a large company selling new homes. I had always enjoyed selling, and this job was the best I'd ever had. So you can imagine my dismay when I noticed I couldn't see the new street signs, which were being put up in the newly developed areas.

"My glasses must be wearing out," I'd say to myself, until I had to literally get out of the car and get right under the signs in order to read them.

One day, while I was previewing some new homes, I could not find a new street. I just couldn't see the new street signs. Finally, I managed to find the one I was looking for. I parked my car in front of the property and proceeded to walk to the back. *The sliding doors should be open*, I thought to myself. As I walked, I could feel the ground wasn't level. What I did not realize was there were many chuck holes which I could not see. My foot went into a hole and I stumbled. To my shock, I realized, not only was I losing my sight, but I had lost my depth perception as well. Somehow, I found my way back to my car and sat there trembling.

I thought to myself, *What's going on with me? I must need new glasses. I can't even read the signs anymore. I'll call an ophthalmologist. I need a specialist.*

Later I made several calls looking for the specialist who could give me some glasses so I could see again. I soon found a doctor who came highly recommended and called for an appointment.

"The first appointment available will be in three and a half months," the receptionist said.

"But I need to see him right now. I think something's really wrong."

"Sorry, ma'am, but we don't have any immediate appointments available at this time. The doctor even works half a day on Saturday trying to get his patients taken care of. I can put you on the cancellation list, but, honestly, unless patients are very sick, they do not cancel or change their appointments."

"Okay, please put me on the list and give me the first appointment possible."

I continued to work very carefully. Luckily, I had scheduled a cruise to the Hawaii islands, which would take two weeks. Now you'd think five ladies on a cruise ship would be having a ball, right? Not me. I felt out of kilter, as if my eyes were disjointed from my head.

One morning as we got ready for breakfast, one of my friends said, "Rose, your make-up looks horrible. It looks like a little old lady put it on. You've got blotches of color on both cheeks and your eye brows are not where they are supposed to be."

I did not notice how poorly I had put my make-up on, until she mentioned it. After that, I became very self-conscious. I suddenly realized I could not see well when I looked into the mirror. I couldn't tell whether I had done a good job or a bad one.

When I got back from my vacation, it was almost time for my appointment with the ophthalmologist. This was a maddening experience. My eyes were dilated, then, I waited in a separate room. After an eternity, they called me in. The doctor looked at my eyes. He stepped back and inhaled deeply.

"I want you to go to Sacramento right now to see a specialist. He is very good, and you need to go immediately. I'll make the appointment."

"I can't go right now in this commute traffic. You've just dilated my eyes, and I'm here by myself."

"Okay, I'll call and set it up for nine in the morning. I want you there."

It was a mystery to me why the doctor was suddenly so concerned, and I was nervous about it. Did I have a good night's sleep? Did I sleep at all? You know what the answer was. Upon awakening, I felt like a slow-moving sloth. Even after two cups of coffee, I was still dragging my tail.

Arriving at the new doctor's office, again my eyes were dilated. This time the new doctor injected me with dye and took pictures while the dye traveled through my eye vessels. Then he left the room to study the film.

"Well?" I asked, as he reentered the room.

"You have what we call macular degeneration."

"What's that?"

He gave me a lengthy explanation as to what it was.

"Okay, so now let's cure it!" I said enthusiastically, although the voice inside my head was screaming in horror.

"There is no cure. You will eventually go blind."

My world stood still. My eyes got larger and larger. I expected them to pop right out of my head.

How can he look at me and tell me I am going blind? I thought. *Doesn't he have anything positive to say? This man is heartless.*

"The good part is, you won't lose all of your vision," he said. "You will still have your peripheral vision."

I pictured myself walking forward with my head turned as far as I could to one side. I'll tell you honestly, that scared me.

"Give me a week to study all the film. Then I'll tell you if there is anything I can do to help you."

This is how I found out about my macular degeneration. Scared? You bet. Defeated? No way. I knew I would soon be out there learning and asking questions. I would not give up!

Through a mutual friend, I learned of a support group in our area. At first I was very reluctant to join a support group. What I did not want was for someone to say, "Poor Rose, you can no longer do what every other person is able to do." Little did I know the support group would enable me to do just that. It opened up a brand new world for me. All I had to do was ask.

**I have learned from experience that
the greater part of our happiness or misery depends on our
dispositions and not our circumstances.
—Martha Washington**

Chapter 5: Lois's Story

My vision problems began about ten years ago. I noticed I couldn't read the newspaper or recipes anymore without using a magnifying glass. I tried several types but couldn't find one strong enough to read numbers in the phone directory.

I made an appointment with my optometrist and asked him if he could please give me stronger glasses.

After the exam, he said, "I can't give you anything to correct your vision. However, I'm going to make an appointment for you with an ophthalmologist for a more thorough examination."

After that doctor's examination, I was shocked when the doctor said, "You have macular degeneration causing your problem."

I said, "What on earth is macular what?" I had no idea what he was talking about.

The doctor went on to explain, "It frequently affects older people. No one has been able to determine the cause, and, much worse, there is no cure for it. However, you are one of the lucky one's, as you have the dry type. It will take you much longer to go blind."

He handed me a grid to tape to my refrigerator to use to check my vision daily.

He added, "Please continue using your artificial tears several times a day as necessary. If the lines on the grid suddenly become more wavy or blurred, call and come in to see me right away. Otherwise, I will see you next year."

All the way home, I was trying to sort this problem out. What on earth would my husband and I do if I did go blind? We lived out in the country, and my husband's driving was hazardous. The picture I had in my mind was moving to town and me sitting on the street corner with a tin cup selling pencils.

When we discussed my problem with the family, we all agreed that, somewhere, there had to be a cure for macular degeneration. We just had to get out and look for it. No way was I going blind.

I made an appointment to consult with a low vision specialist. Same story! This specialist explained more about the problem.

"We just don't know what is causing this problem, so therefore we don't know what to do for it. Some of my patients eat spinach at least three times a week and drink a glass of red wine every day. They seem to think it slows the disease down somewhat. Why don't you try this and continue using your eye drops? It won't cure anything but just may help you."

I realized there were no guarantees, but I was certainly willing to try. I ate spinach every which way I could fix it until I'm sure my eyeballs were turning green. I'm still puzzled as to why Popeye had such good results from spinach. I have never been a big fan of wine, so I drank red grape juice instead. Could I see any better? No. Maybe it was the grape juice.

I read everything I could find on macular degeneration. All of the theories on possible relief, I tried. After about three years of gradual loss of vision, it seemed to slow down. My vision stayed about the same for two years. I decided it might be all the vitamins I was taking. I was not only taking a lot of vitamins, I also took ginko biloba, lutein, and bilberry. And, of course, I ate spinach. It was either that, or I was on the right page with the good Lord above.

After about two years of thinking I had solved my problems, my vision started to fade again. I couldn't read addresses or road signs. I would circle the block several times and even then had to park to go closer to check the address. I had to continue to drive, as my husband was unable to drive anymore. If my neighbors had realized how poor my vision was, I'm sure they would have stayed off the road whenever they saw me driving.

After my husband died, I felt isolated, so I moved to town to be closer to my son. It was there that I read about the support group for the visually impaired which met every month. Believe me, it took a lot of courage to take that first step. I was shaking when I quietly slipped into the back row. There were at least fifty people there, all with the same problem as mine. As soon as the meeting was over, I slipped out of the back door without talking to anyone.

Later, after the shock wore off, I decided, since it really wasn't so bad, maybe I should go back the next month. I did go the next month, met the leader who was completely blind, and slowly started coming out of my shell. The meetings were inspirational. They offered demonstrations of all the aids available and had speakers giving us encouragement. I decided, *This is the way to go. It won't cure me, but I could learn to live a normal life. Maybe, at least, I could throw away the tin cup!*

I was doing so much better mentally, but soon I had to have back surgery. Kaiser Hospital's spine clinic in Roseville, California, was going to pose a difficult transportation problem. My daughter lived several miles away from it in Granite Bay and was going to drive all the way to Lodi, a journey of more than 85 miles roundtrip, to pick me up for all my appointments in Roseville. The best solution, we decided, was to sell our homes, buy one closer to Kaiser, and move in together. It was a wise move for both of us.

My family was very supportive of me, both with my back and vision problems. I was becoming more dependent on them all the time. Believe me after my surgery that changed. I think it may have been after my daughter had to empty my bedpan for a few days. Although I sincerely appreciated all the concern and help, but I knew this had to change. I was losing my independence, and I wasn't ready for the rocking chair and soap operas.

My daughter encouraged me to exercise and do things for myself. I started cooking and doing housework. It seemed to me the house wasn't getting very dirty anymore, until the kids reminded me I was getting as blind as a bat. I really didn't mind since they say bats can find food a mile away. At least I wouldn't starve.

I lived just a few blocks from the Senior Center, so I started playing bingo twice a week. I signed up for a writing class to write my memoirs. Later, there was a computer class available. The center was starting a support group for the vision impaired, so I joined. After a couple of months, our leader died, and no one was willing to volunteer for the job. I agreed to help as long as everyone was willing to help me.

This brought me to my first encounter with Rose, and I must say it has been an amazing experience. Rose has such a great sense of humor. You sneeze, she laughs; you trip and fall, she will pick you up, then laughs.

She can see something good in everyone. Well, actually she can't see, but she is always willing to share her feelings.

At one of our meetings we had several staff members from the Society for the Blind for a discussion on their senior intensive retreat. Eight of our members signed on for the retreat, including Rose and me. Believe me when I tell you our lives were irrevocably changed for the better.

The moment avoiding failure becomes your motivator, you're down the path of inactivity. You stumble, only if you're moving.
—Anonymous

Chapter 6: Our Journey Begins
(As Told by Lois)

We got over the first challenging bump in the road when we were finally able to accept the fact we were going blind. It's a one-way street, and we knew there was no turning back. So, we began to charge ahead. We joined the support group to gain knowledge and share our problems with others. We are determined to make the most of what we'd learn to better our lives.

Counselors—totally blind counselors—spoke at an Insight meeting in Roseville explaining the many benefits of participating in a retreat they were conducting. It was for one week, and transportation would be provided. They assured us we would be well cared for. We couldn't complain about the cost since everything was free. All we needed to do was sign up, pack enough clothes for a week, and be ready when the van arrived. Simple and inviting! I decided maybe I'd take a book and writing tablet along so in my spare time I could write a few letters. Actually I secretly wanted to have my dream vacation—one which I had never really had taken in my life.

The day to begin the retreat was soon upon us. Several times we questioned whether we were doing the right thing. It was a chance in a lifetime, so how could we go wrong? Our families could always pick us up if we got sick. The driver of the van called the day before to tell each of us the exact time he would be picking us up. It was too late now to back out.

A good-looking, friendly young man arrived within fifteen minutes of the designated time. He was very efficient and made us feel so welcome. By the way, he wasn't blind.

There was one little shy woman already on the van when I got on. She looked as frightened as we felt. As each person was picked up, introductions were made, and the van soon became very noisy. By the time we arrived at the home of the retreat, we were old friends, laughing and joking around.

Our home for the week was a large home in a very nice residential area. We were directed into the house and assigned our rooms. Rose and I were assigned a downstairs bedroom since we had difficulties climbing stairs. We then stood helplessly by as we watched in awe while blind staff members carried our luggage to each of our rooms. They ran up and down the stairs and never missed a step. Our new friend who was so shy was assigned the bedroom next to ours downstairs. She may have had second thoughts after all the talking and laughing that went on that first night. Finally, we went to sleep, but Rose certainly breathed heavily. To this day, she still won't admit she snores.

Once everyone was acquainted with his and her rooms and roommates, we were directed to the kitchen. We were told to make our own sandwiches for dinner. What? No room service? We ate and chatted away expecting to call it a day. We seemed to forget this was called an intensive retreat.

As soon as we all swallowed our last bite of food we were directed to the patio. There we were each given our own canes. The canes were specifically fitted to us with individual identifications since they were to be our constant companions. Along with the canes, we were given blinders or shades, which we would be wearing throughout the training so we could learn in total darkness.

Following several hours of introducing us to our canes, it was getting late. We thought it was our bedtime, but, instead, we all gathered in the family room for a fireside discussion with the staff. There we learned of our schedule for the week. I could see letter writing was out for this week. More importantly, I wondered, how could we possibly cram all of that knowledge in our heads in just one week?

Activities were well planned so that, each day, we progressed gradually. By the end of the week, we could look back and understand how each step had advanced us to our final outcomes.

These fireside gatherings became a very important part of our schedule. We were divided into three groups, each with a counselor and usually a mentor. We would be alternating our assignments as we went.

We could soon identify each person's personality. Our little shy partner blossomed. She was soon chatting away as she joined us in our room every night. *If you can't fight them, join them,* she decided. She had been very depressed when she arrived but soon found out she wasn't alone. She soaked up all the information like a sponge. She took home with her the confidence she gained knowing there is so much help out there. All she had to do was ask for it.

We had two male "jokers" in the crowd and believe me one joke led to another. These two men had actually been very depressed over their situation at first. The fireside discussion along with the laughter and humor changed them over night. There was never a dull moment. By the end of the retreat, they were ready to conquer the world.

One of the ladies was nearly totally blind and her family, bless their hearts, were killing her with kindness. They would not let her do anything for herself. She learned so much, as we all did, about how independent we could be. Her family members attended our graduation and were surprised to learn that perhaps they had been hurting her, rather than helping.

Everyone had an opportunity to express his or her feelings. The counselors were a great inspiration. Whether we felt depression and hopelessness or saw macular degeneration as just another challenge in our lives, we had our chance to unload our feelings of sorrow and anger.

Through these group discussions we learned so much. Every night we would put marbles in a bowl, one for each thing we learned that day. That bowl was full of marbles by the end of the week.

Actually there was only one complaint we heard during the week and we heard it often from Rose.

"I'm extremely exhausted!" she said. We all, indeed, did agree with her.

We can only encourage everyone to seek help if you are having a loss of vision. Remember, you are not alone. This intensive retreat is a chance in a lifetime to turn your lives around. You do not have to stumble through life when there are so many opportunities available.

One does not discover new lands without consenting to lose sight of the shore for a very long time.
—Andre Gide

Chapter 7: Our Friend, the Cane

We were assigned our own specific cane, since it was important to get the right type and length to meet our individual needs.

We were surprised to find there are many types of canes. Some women prefer folding canes, because they are convenient to carry in their purses. However, these canes are not as substantial as the long white canes. Many people utilize a stationery walking cane for balance and support. We advise you to get the long white cane with the metal tip. It is much easier to identify the objects in your path using the sound of the metal tip.

The length of the cane is very important. If you are six feet tall or over, you certainly don't want a three-foot cane for obvious reasons. The rule of the thumb is the cane should reach between your nose and your eyebrows.

The cane should be flexible enough to bend some. For example, if you are walking and come across a ridge or crack in the sidewalk, your cane should stop you. Not to the point it causes you to stop on a dime, but it should be flexible and bends but does not break.

Why should the cane be so long? The cane is used with a sweeping motion about three feet in front of you. Sweeping the area, you may suddenly feel something. Simply anchor your cane and walk up to it so you can then identify the object in front of you.

Imagine, if you will, you are walking in the hills above the Grand Canyon, and all of a sudden you feel nothing in front of you. You need time to stop. If you had a short cane and you had only one step in front of you, you might just go down the embankment. So, by circling the cane at least three feet ahead, you will be able to stop in time.

The cane, we were told, would become the most important part of our lives, so we were taught how to use them properly. Holding our hand at waste level, we opened the palm facing up so the cane will rest there. We found we could control it by revolving our fingers. When we encountered an obstacle, we could then feel it against our bodies.

When we were in the house or in a crowd outside, we found it was best to use the pencil grip on the handle so the cane would be directly in front of us. We didn't want to trip anyone or cause a major pile up.

Using the cane takes practice and that is exactly what we had at the retreat, lots and lots of it in all different situations. We learned how important the cane is to help us in our daily lives. It should be automatic that we reach for the cane every morning.

It's just as important as putting on our shoes and socks each day.

Since our cane would be our best friend, we thought perhaps we should name them. There were so many complimentary, funny and positive names given. So much better than calling it our white stick.

Rose immediately named her cane "Coffee Bean." Why did she call it that? One of the many stories that stuck in her mind was, "What do you want to be, a carrot, egg, or a coffee bean?" This sounds like a silly comparison, but our teacher proceeded to tell this story in her calm, sweet voice:

"You want to be a carrot? When they put you in hot water, you will get all soft and mushy. Or would you rather be an egg—hard-boiled and tough? Or would you rather be a coffee bean? When it gets in hot water, it projects a pleasant aroma and boils into a delicious drink, which is almost always in demand."

It's no wonder Rose, with her upbeat personality, named her cane "Coffee Bean."

Lois named her cane "Cane and Able." Using her friendly cane enabled her to go about her business. It was definitely not a stick or a crutch!

Every tomorrow has two handles. We can take hold of it with the handle of anxiety or the handle of faith.
—Henry Ward Beecher

Chapter 8 – Computer and Braille

Our days were divided into three segments, giving us two hours with each class. We rotated subjects daily: cane travel followed by computer and Braille and, last but not least, homemaking.

Now when it was our turn on the computer, Rose understood more because she had more experience with computers. They might as well have been talking to a blank wall trying to get through to Lois. However, we didn't get too discouraged because we knew the purpose of the class was to determine if we needed further training.

We were introduced to everything that was available to help us in our daily living. There was Dragon Naturally Speaking, a program that will do the typing for us on the computer as we talk into a microphone.

Using a closed captioned TV allowed us to enlarge fonts (typing letters) so we were able to enlarge whatever we wanted to read. Some of the technology, especially those that magnified fonts large enough for us to read almost anything, made us feel great. We were back in connection with the world. *Too bad they couldn't drive a car for us*, we thought.

The scanner was another aid that can scan the printed word and read to us when we no longer can see at all.

The majority of our lessons were often demonstrated on the Jaws program. With this program we do not need vision because it talks to us as we are typing so we will know what we have typed. Jaws also allows us to surf the Internet using keyboard commands instead of a mouse. It converts the text on a Web page into a computerized voice that comes out through a speaker. Accessing the Internet through Jaws makes it easy to do banking, buy plane tickets, or go shopping for groceries and music.

One of the most fascinating gadgets we were introduced to gave directions to us while we were walking. It's like using a personal global positioning system. We simply gave it the address where we wanted to go. It guided us there and brought us safely home again.

We were both so fascinated with the gadgets. Rose wondered, "How on earth do they work?"

Lois just shook her head. "I can't even program my VCR, so I could never explain them to you!" she said, giving Rose a playful shove.

We realized both during and after the classes we were really in need of some one-on-one training. We were told about classes available at the Society for the Blind. First we'd have to go through the California Department of Rehabilitation to be qualified for this service. They then would arrange for the classes and transportation at no cost to us.

As if we weren't confused enough with the computer, we were next moved into the Braille class.

"Now this might be more my style of writing: one peg at a time," Lois commented.

Have you ever tried to read Braille? For us, we found it to be just like any foreign language we'd tried. It's confusing at first, but once you get the hang of it, it's amazingly simple.

Using one block of wood with six holes in it and six pegs to fit the holes, we learned to spell out the whole alphabet, one letter at a time, as well as numbers. Of course, as we advanced, we soon learned short cuts and contractions. Without those, it could take us a week filling up two or three tablets by writing one letter at a time.

Being slow learners, we were just thrilled to be able to write our names.

ROSE was

LOIS was

Braille may be a mystery to most of us, but it's a blessing to the blind. Is Braille really worth our time to learn? Ask a totally blind person. It is an extremely important tool, and you will find it will inform us about the world around us when we no longer can see. It provides alternative reading and writing, plus special benefits such as labeling spices, cans of food, and all the food in freezers and refrigerator, not to mention marking clothes so we are able to coordinate colors and styles. Imagine the strange looks we'd get if we showed up with brown slacks, chartreuse blouses and red polka dot socks.

Mastering Braille required us to make a commitment to learn, and we found great benefit by working with a partner who rebutted each of our lame excuses for not wanting to even try.

"I'm too old to learn."

"I have no feeling in my fingers."

"My fingers are too big, so I can't feel one dot at a time."

The trick to overcoming resistance to learning Braille is to be determined to learn. That, and practice, practice, practice! Start with three or four letters at a time; it may take several weeks to master these. After you have conquered these, then move on to four more. If you can't feel with your index finger, try another finger. Cut your nails short so you can use the very tip of your finger. Or sprinkle a little talcum powder on them so they will slide easily. It isn't going to be a piece of cake, but once learned the benefits of Braille are astronomical.

Just imagine giving a lecture with no noticeable notes. Your speech is written in Braille on a card in your pocket so you can talk as you read.

Also, when shopping, you will discover many stores are identified in Braille on the outside panel at the entrance. The elevators are marked, as well as public bathroom doors. Have you ever been aware of this before?

There are free Braille classes available that will provide lessons over the phone or in the mail. For information, contact the Society for the Blind in your area. The Hadley School for the Blind is one source with on-line registration.

Remember, it is positive thinking that leads you on and sheer determination that gets you where you want to be!

Braille Chart

Braille Alphabet:

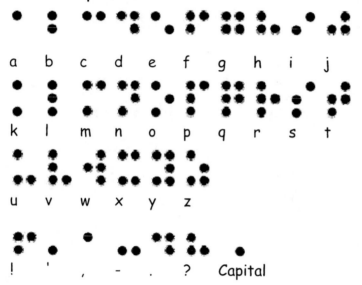

a   b   c   d   e   f   g   h   i   j

k   l   m   n   o   p   q   r   s   t

u   v   w   x   y   z

!   '   ,   -   .   ?   Capital

Numbers:

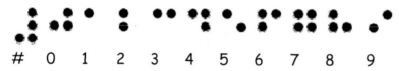

\#   0   1   2   3   4   5   6   7   8   9

Never eat more than you can lift.
—Miss Piggy

Chapter 9: Homemaking

Our homemaking segment of training could have been called "making our house a home." We were shown various ways to enjoy our house and allow it to fulfill our lives. If we had any preconceived ideas about cooking without our shades on, we were in for a surprise.

Our instructor was totally blind. This was difficult to believe because she floated around the kitchen with complete confidence. Although we were following a blind person, we were the ones feeling blind, since our first requirement was for everyone to put on light-blocking shades. We thought, if we could learn to be half as confident as she, it'd be certainly worth the effort.

Our first menu included chef's salad and garlic bread. We were given cutting boards and chef's knives, not table knives, mind you. We were instructed to place the knife on the top of the cutting board with the sharp edge facing away from us, and the handle to the right. Scary? You bet it was!

We quickly realized we should keep the conversation on the up side. We didn't want anyone getting upset and sounding off with that knife in his or her hand. This could be why there was always so much laughter coming from the kitchen at meal preparation time. Our meals tasted delicious, and we didn't find a finger, or even a fingernail, in any of our food.

Following its preparation, our food was lined up on the serving table ready to be served. First we put on our required shades, then held our cane in the left armpit (for right-handed people). We wrapped our napkins around our silverware, which we then put in our pockets. The plate was held in our left hands supported on the table. With the back of our right hands, we located the serving dishes. In serving ourselves, we placed the food at 12 o'clock on our plate and gradually rotated our plate as we traveled down the line. We learned to tell just how much food we were getting by feeling the weight of the dish. The last item we received was the bread or roll to use as a pusher. A pusher is a helper we use to direct the food onto the fork or spoon.

Once we found a vacant chair at the table, we were given our choice of drinks. With soda we received a glass with ice. We learned to hold our fingers over the top edge of the glass so we could feel when the glass was full. Another trick of the trade.

Now to enjoy the food, right? Have you ever eaten an empty fork? We tried and tried until it was so funny and we were so hungry. We finally realized what the pusher was for. Did we miss our mouths and spill any? Food was all over our laps and on the floor, but we soon got the hang of it. The seeing-eye dogs resting under the table didn't care much for the salad, but certainly enjoyed rice and other tasty morsels.

Each day we had a variety of food, all delicious, and we could eat all we wanted. Later during the week, we were told, once we cleaned our plates, we could go back for seconds without our shades on. Good thing they didn't tell us that the first day!

Homemaking didn't stop with food preparation, although you can tell where our hearts were—right above our stomachs.

Organizing the kitchen was another subject we covered because it is critical to avoid mishaps in our kitchens. Convenience is the secret to organizing. Placing the appliances we use daily near an electrical outlet, with the cord secure in the back, is important. It is helpful if our electrical outlets and appliances are a contrasting color from the counter. If not, we may want to get covers for the appliances, which will make them easier to identify.

This is also a good time to talk about identifying the buttons on our appliances. Raised dots, Braille markings, rubber bands, magnets, and brightly colored fingernail polish can all be very useful and serve a purpose, not only in our kitchens, but all through the house. For example, we may put one rubber band around a can of corn, and two on a can of peas. Or we may use bright pink nail polish to indicate the "on" button on an appliance.

Marking our spices and condiments is important because many of us have worn out our sense of smell. Chili powder in your oatmeal cookies wouldn't taste very good so it's best to use large letters to identify spices. For example, cut out a large capital "A" and attach it to a container of allspice with scotch tape. Use "B" on basil, "C" for cinnamon, etc. Actually, since we have been encouraging everyone to use Braille, the spice cabinet alone would be a good place to start putting it to use.

Another suggestion would be to use red nail polish to paint letters on top of a can. For example, paint "T" for tomatoes. We sometimes use the computer to make large alphabet letters, print them out, and scotch tape them on. This is very inexpensive and gives us a feeling of accomplishment.

Choose long-handled spoons and measuring cups whenever you can. It is so much easier to scoop and level instead of pour when you are no longer able to see. Usually the measurements on these utensils are in raised letters, but, if not, they can be highlighted with nail polish. There are also spoons on the market that are already bent so that we can dip them in spice containers and level off without spilling. Someone is constantly coming up with new ideas to make our lives much simpler.

Learn to identify shapes and sizes of packaging. Keeping items separated, you can use rubber bands to identify cans of food. Better yet, go back to using Braille so you can mark food expiration dates as well.

Be consistent. Make sure that you and everyone in the family place items in the kitchen in the same location every time.

Beware! Your refrigerator can be the breeding grounds for green and fuzzy foods. Store your foods in separate, well-marked compartments. You can always add more storage bins so everything has a special place. Milk and other liquids should be kept on the top shelf with the open containers in front. Use the door shelves for condiments, making sure to use the same shelf every time.

Label, code and separate foods so they are always located in the same place. Use Braille, large letters, or color codes for identification.

Cookbooks are available in large print materials, Braille, and audio tapes. Collecting all the items you will need before you begin cooking will save you time when you are preparing a meal. To avoid confusion, gather your ingredients together, keeping like items apart, and place them in a pan until you need them.

If you need to preheat the oven, marking the temperature controls will help. Most local utility companies will provide oven and stove control dials in large print or in Braille. Mark frequently used settings on these dials with contrasting colors.

Use these markings on dishwashers, microwave ovens, and washer and driers.

Another hint for safety is to use elbow-length oven mitts. Use pots and pans with built-in spouts, making it easier to pour and serve.

We had so much information crowded into our heads during the intensive retreat. Each night we had our fireside evaluation of all that day's activities. As an added advantage, some of us kept a diary each night so we could refer to it once we returned home to our old ways.

Our homemaking skills didn't stop with the kitchen. Other daily tasks included shopping, paying bills, writing checks, and keeping track of money in our billfolds. We had lessons in changing light bulbs, replacing fuses, and even hanging pictures on the wall with our shades on. We threaded needles, sewed buttons on, and were even lucky enough to try out the new voting machines.

All of these activities gave us a wonderful chance to learn new ways of doing routine things, like the class we had on personal hygiene and cosmetics. We soaked up all the information we could possibly remember and then some.

The retreat was very well planned. Each day gifted us with a new advanced experience. Please don't ever miss a chance to attend one. It is not only an opportunity of a lifetime but a chance to make new friends and share experiences mixed with lots of fun, laughter, and ideas.

Courage is resistance to fear, mastery of fear, not absence of fear.
—Mark Twain

Chapter 10: Mobile Training

Remember our friend, the cane, we were introduced to at the beginning of our journey? It had brought us a long way toward building self-reliance.

By properly using the long white cane, we were now walking with confidence. We no longer had to walk with our heads bent down, hoping to identify anything in our path. We could hold our heads up high to send a message out to others that we can be and are, indeed, independent.

Many people stay confined to their homes because of their fear of being hurt. With the thorough training we had at our retreat, we felt confident there wasn't really anything we couldn't do and do it safely.

We learned to shoreline on the sidewalk by using the tip of the cane, letting it find the edges of the walkway. We soon learned to identify driveways, curbs, and any bumps in the road.

We used this knowledge on our first trip going to Starbucks. You can imagine the thrill we felt using our cane skills, locating the entrance and using our gift of smell, knowing we were in the right place.

Using our pencil grip on the cane, we managed to find the end of the line. Did we tell you we were still wearing our shades?

We ordered our drinks, moved to the next window to pick them up, and followed directions to the nearest table. Wow, what a thrill, and no one spilled a drop!

Our next challenge was a trip to the California State Fair in Sacramento. Walking was a big challenge, but then we were allowed to remove our shades, part of the time.

Our first place of interest was the livestock barns. The big pigs were out for water and feed. Some of the people in our group were in their path as they were being led back to their pens. The pigs just didn't understand we were blind, so there was a lot of squealing going on. It was hard to tell whether it was the pigs or we girls.

All of us, with our long white canes and shades, located the horse show. The look of concern, we were told, on everyone's face was better than the horse show. We're sure there were some people in the crowd wondering, if we were really blind, what were we doing there. Maybe we just needed a rest.

With each day, we became more confident in the use of our canes. We were sent to the grocery store with a shopping list to do some grocery buying for dinner. We learned almost every store has a personal shopper who will help us, if we asked in advance. We used the pencil grip with our cane and pulled the cart behind us. We knew when we were in the produce department by the mist we felt, the aroma of the fresh fruit, and the feel of the vegetables.

Then, we proceeded to the check out counter with our cart full of nutritious, healthy items. The clerk rang up the items, which totaled $24.76. We looked at our instructor and said, "It's your turn now." The clerk laughed as we pulled off our shades and explained what we were doing.

We decided being blind wasn't so bad after all. The canes and the shades we were wearing garnered a lot of attention from the public. Many asked about our program, with some wanting to get a job at the Society. Others knew of a family member or friend who was vision impaired and could benefit by this training.

Our cane travel became easier each day as we learned to let the cane do the walking. We tuned in to the little messages it was sending us.

It was Thursday already. We are on the road early for another big day. We arrived at Arden Fair Shopping Mall, in Sacramento, around eight in the morning, before the stores opened. We practiced our shore-lining skills along corridors first so we'd be ready when the stores opened. We had no problems finding See's Candy Store. Our noses guide us to the wonderful chocolate aroma.

We each paid for our own purchase using the skills we were taught. In our billfold we learned to identify money by leaving the one dollar bills straight, the five dollars bills folded in half, the tens folded in thirds, and the twenty's in half lengthwise. If our purchase was under ten dollars, we gave the clerk a bill folded in thirds and said, "I'm giving you a ten dollar bill." Then the clerk would count out the returned amount.

Then we asked the clerk for directions to another store. He gave us verbal directions, and we had no problems locating it by shore-lining the building.

You can't imagine how rewarding it was to find the store all by ourselves. Of course, our guardian angels were with us all the way, even though they were totally blind themselves. Guardian angels were what we called our instructors and helpers.

We discovered on the side panel of the store entrance the name of the store is written in Braille. Another reason to learn Braille! The elevators are also marked in Braille on each side of the door opening.

Being able to see for most of our lives, we realized we had neglected our other senses. We learned to be more alert by using our senses of smell and hearing.

Our biggest challenge was still to come. We could hear the escalators just ahead of us and couldn't believe our teachers wanted us to use them, yet it was remarkable how

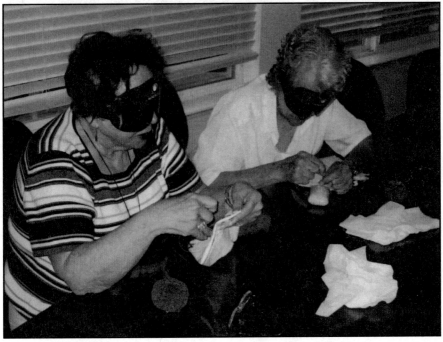

Top: Rose and Lois checking out at the grocery store
Bottom: Sewing buttons, wearing their shades

Top: Rose at the Farmer's Market
Bottom: Lois lunching at a public restaurant

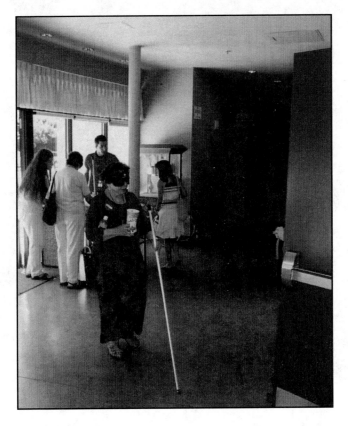

Top: Rose and Lois; one of their lighter moments "without shades"
Bottom: Rose entering the theater to see "Grease"

Top: Lois walking through the tunnel at Amtrak
Bottom: Our Vacuum Cleaner worked wonders after meals

easy it was to conquer that fear. We felt for the railing, which moved upward. Then using the pencil grip on the cane, we placed the tip on the entrance, feeling the clicks as the escalator moved. Counting one, two, and three, we stepped out, following our canes and hanging on to the rail, since the escalator did the rest.

Once at the top, we felt our canes telling us it was the end. Going down was just the opposite. Nobody got hurt, although Rose wasn't quite so enthused as Lois.

A personal note from Rose:

"I was scared to death. All my life, I have been a little hesitant when stepping on and off any escalator. And they wanted me to do it with shades, all by myself? I pictured my feet taking off and leaving my body behind. I knew my feet would get to the top, but where was the rest of my body?

"I rarely perspire, but I could feel my hands accumulating lots of moisture. My breathing was shallow. I could not speak. I thought, *Whatever happens, will just have to happen.* By the grace of God, I got to the top, hearing voices yelling, 'You made it.'

"But now I had to come down! One way or another, I knew *I would end at the bottom!* I could not speak. I could feel my chest expanding and contracting. I whispered to myself, *Here goes nothing.* Then, within seconds, I was at the bottom.

Many voices were cheering, 'Good job, Rose.' Can you imagine they even clapped for me?

"Being the first to try it, I was not aware there were teachers and helpers all around me. There was one in front, and another behind guiding me. They made sure I was not going to hurt myself, but I didn't know it at the time.

"Looking back, I realized I generated my fear all by myself. This is what we do to ourselves when we don't know what is going to happen next. By attending the retreats, I no longer am afraid to go up and down the escalators. However, I still respect them and use caution, which is a smart thing for everyone to do."

There were extra special surprises on our agenda, each a learning experience. Again, we had our shades on most of the time.

We were fortunate to attend the musical, *Grease*. Yes, wearing our shades, we went into the theater and found our seats. After we got settled, we were allowed to take them off and enjoy the performance, which brought back many happy memories.

What happened to the days of the week? Today was Friday already. We were facing another busy day. Early in the morning we toured the Society for the Blind. The Society has so much to offer anyone with visual problems. Many of the services are free to those who are legally blind, so there is absolutely no excuse for anyone to sit home feeling sorry for herself or himself.

We were warned ahead of time we would be eating lunch at the Fresh Choice Buffet, canes and shades required. We each had our guardian angel telling us what was on the menu. We helped ourselves to whatever we wanted and later were required to go through the line again for either a second helping or dessert. We ate in the regular dining room area with no fear of making a mess. Well, almost. We learned the hard way how to keep the food on our plates by using a bread roll for a pusher. We didn't look back to see how much food was under the table.

We had to use the powder room before we went any further. This was a real learning experience. The eerie feeling of complete and utter darkness in a closed room was overwhelming.

Another personal note from Rose:

When I stepped into the toilette stall, I reached out to lock the door. I felt awkward because I knew or felt I was the only one in there. Everything felt pitch dark. You are probably asking, what does *dark* feel like? A feeling came over me as if I were at the bottom of a well. It became difficult to breath, not knowing if I was facing the door or the porcelain facility. I propped my cane against the corner, hoping it would not fall down.

I was beginning to panic and said a little prayer asking for guidance, adding a postscript asking that as I completed my mission and walked out, there'd be no evidence as to where I had been.

To complete our day, we toured the Sacramento Railroad Museum. We identified many of the features of the trains, walking up the stairs and through the dining and mail cars. Oh, how we loved our canes first getting up and then coming down the stairs. It felt like the canes could actually see better than we could. Remember, we were wearing our shades.

Saturday was graduation day—the day to share our accomplishments with our family and friends. When we had graduated in the past, there always seemed to be mixed emotions. This graduation was no different.

We were all quite proud of our many accomplishments, but sad to know the week we spent with these good friends had come to a close. We exchanged hugs and had private little conversations with each other, expressing our hopes our paths would cross again. The next time we would be far better informed and more confident than the first day of this retreat.

Thank goodness for tissues because many of us had instant colds, which meant tears in the eyes and running noses. We had absorbed a world of knowledge as well as made many new friends.

We arrived home exhausted but eager to share our experiences and go out and conquer the world.

Success is getting what you want. Happiness is wanting what you get.
— Anonymous

Chapter 11: Back Home Again

Graduation day had been more than a day of thank-you's and good-byes. It was a time to count our blessings.

We had completed a week of learning and training that was going to make our lives much easier and enjoyable. All of it was free of charge, thanks to the Society for the Blind. As we left to go home, we took with us far more self-assurance than we brought with us. You just can't imagine the emotions we all felt. The confidence we had gained to become more independent and self-sufficient was evident. We could sense the accomplishment as everyone departed with his or her trusted canes, heads held high.

We arrived home, as promised, safe and sound. As we entered the door to our homes, everything looked so much friendlier and brighter. We were no longer seeing just four walls that made us feel like we were prisoners in our own homes. Even though our beds were certainly comforting, we found we missed the chatter and laughter of our retreat buddies.

The time was now to get our message out and share our renewed enthusiasm for life with the world. As we made our plans for our coming support group meeting, everyone was asked to share their feelings and their experience of the retreat. Could it be better and was it worth taking one week out of our lives? What an impact all the energy and enthusiasm had on our support group.

Rose and Lois are now on a mission to spread the word, HOPE! Even though we are blind, we are definitely human, with the same dreams and desires we have always had. We breathe, we eat—oh do we ever eat—we sleep, we laugh, we cry, and do just about everything everyone is capable of doing. We just need to use different methods to get our needs met and our goals accomplished.

We no longer are subject to frustration because we have now been empowered to interact with others. Everything begins with believing in ourselves. If we continually said to others, "Oh I can't do this or that because I can't see," we would soon believe our self-talk and give up trying. However, if we said, "I have a little problem. Just give me time to work this out. I know I can do it, it just may take me a little longer!" we develop the confidence to try new things. It's truly the "Power of Positive Thinking."

There is much work being done on macular degeneration research these days, and we believe, every year, scientists come closer to finding the cause and cure for macular degeneration and other vision problems. Often we see people with vision loss feeling depressed, helpless, and hopeless, bemoaning the fact they can't function in their daily lives. We believe if they continued these negative thoughts, they may never be able to improve their situation.

We know from experience the first bump in the road is the roughest. Talking to others with similar problems will do wonders for your outlook on life. You are not alone. There are more and more every day joining us in our loss of vision, a journey out of sight. Never give up hope that we may someday have a cure. After all, anything is possible.

We encourage you to join a support group in your area where you can share your story and problems with others. Through these discussion groups, you will hear how others have coped with the same problem. Look beyond your loss and accept it as just another challenge in your life to overcome.

You will realize how much you can learn by listening, feeling and smelling! Yes, you may first go through several phases of grief, including denial, bargaining, anger, depression and, then finally, acceptance. Take these steps, one at a time, in your own personal time. Embrace each step before going on to the next. Believe it or not, there is a grand new world waiting for you.

We are challenging you to open the door to all the opportunities waiting for you. Let life become fun and exciting again. It doesn't really take much effort to enjoy it—just a willingness to.

Please sign up with others to attend a Senior Intensive Retreat offered through the Society for the Blind and see what it can do for you!

Life goes on for us since we have been practicing all the talents we developed in housekeeping, shopping, and traveling with our trusted canes. Our support group has expanded, and we have kept busy bringing speakers and new ideas to the meetings. With each meeting, we walk away with more knowledge.

We were still energized when we received an invitation to attend an advanced retreat at the Society for the Blind. We were to get more training and wondered how we could possibly absorb more wisdom. We were in for a pleasant surprise, which we will happily share with you next.

Life is either a daring adventure or nothing. To keep our faces toward change and behave like free spirits in the presence of fate is strength undefeatable.
—Helen Keller

Chapter 12: Helen Keller's Story

We would like to share with you a message from Helen Keller's autobiography, *The Story of My Life*, because the example she set has had a big impact on our lives.

Helen Keller was born a normal, healthy child, but at nineteen months old she was stricken with an extremely high fever. She recovered from the fever but had been robbed of her sight and hearing.

In 1887, three months before her seventh birthday, she was introduced to her teacher and very good friend, Anne Mansfield Sullivan.

Helen wrote that on the afternoon of March 2, 1887, she stood on the porch, dumb and not knowing what to expect. She could feel something special was happening because of all the movement. Finding her way to the door opening, she breathed in the lovely fragrance of honeysuckle. She reached out and picked a blossom and smelled it, not knowing what it was.

Helen said, "Anger and bitterness had prayed upon me continually for weeks and a deep languor had succeeded this passionate struggle."

Can't you feel the turmoil this little girl must have gone through? Not knowing what was happening, yet feeling something was. You can almost feel the confusion taking place in her little body.

Helen felt approaching footsteps and reached out her hand, thinking it was her mother. Instead, someone took her hand and drew her in close to her. Helen's reaction was so touching: "I was caught up and held close in the arms of her who had come to reveal all things to me, and more than all things else, to love me."

The morning after her teacher arrived, she led Helen into her room and gave her a doll the little blind children at the Perkins Bridgman had sent.

About the doll, Helen wrote: "Laura Bridgman had dressed it, but I did not know this until later. When I had played with it a little while, Miss Sullivan slowly spelled into my hand the word "d-o-l-l." I was at once interested in this finger play and tried to imitate it. When I finally succeeded in making the letters correctly I was flushed with childish pleasure and pride. Running downstairs to my mother I held up my hand and made the letters for doll. I did not know that I was even spelling a word or even that words existed; I was simply making fingers go in monkeylike imitation. In the days that followed, I learned to do in this un-comprehending way a great many words; among them pin, hat, cup, and a few verbs like sit, stand and walk. My teacher had been with me several weeks before I understood that everything had a name."

We highly recommend you read this inspirational story. Discover how Helen's powerful recognition of water opened her senses and set her sailing onto the sea of knowledge.

Helen Keller wrote several books and received many honors, including the Presidential Medal of Freedom. She did not accomplish all she did by herself. She had many helping hands guiding her along the way—helping hands such as the American Foundation for the Blind or AFB. The words have changed a little today, but their mission remains the same, "To expand possibilities for people with vision loss and achieve equality of access and opportunity that will ensure freedom of choice in our lives."

The American Foundation for the Blind, an organization highly supported and endorsed by Helen Keller, gives each of us a reality check, enabling each of the more than ten million blind and vision impaired to better their lives. People who are severally impaired never know their hidden strengths until they are treated like normal human beings and encouraged to shape their own destinies. The AFB offers resources to help you tap into your own undefeatable inner strengths.

**Knowledge is power,
but enthusiasm throws the switch.
—Anonymous**

Chapter 13: Advanced Retreat

Hi-ho, hi-ho, it's off to another retreat we go! With our trusted canes tapping in front of us, and a spring in our step, we were raring to go.

This advanced session was drastically different from our first retreat when all we could hear was the dragging of our feet.

We were eager to climb into the van and get on board to see what could possibly be in store for us. The six new people we met were all graduates from previous retreats. We felt like these were part of our family we had not seen for a long time.

Right away we decided our group name would be "The Charming Two Timers." Very appropriate, we unanimously agreed, with lots of jokes and laughter.

The same great staff greeted us and assigned our rooms. Just as before, we shared a downstairs bedroom. It wasn't our vision keeping us off the stairs, and it couldn't be our age. It must have been our navigation was rather slow, with our extra baggage and arthritis, tagging along.

We both passed the training we had received on the steps, with shades on, at the first retreat. We really may have been able to go up and down the steps this second time around, but there wasn't enough time for the staff to wait for us every day. Sounds logical, doesn't it?

The roommate in the adjacent room was a mentor we had met at our basic session, so she was quite aware of what nonsense was in store for her. She was in training with us and, sure enough, we had lots of laughter coming from our end of the house all week.

Our first day at the advanced retreat was similar to the first one, with welcoming from the staff and getting acquainted over self- served sandwiches. Once we finished eating, a refresher class on cane travel followed. At our fireside meeting, the counselors laid out the agenda for the week. *Wait a minute, there was no way we could get everything done*, we thought. They suggested the best way was to get right to bed since we'd be getting up early and running non-stop.

Remember the shore-lining class we discussed before? We were briefed again the first morning on how shore-lining would help us to navigate safely. We used the tip of the cane either at ten o'clock or two o'clock to locate the edges of the sidewalk. We felt the lawn on one side so assumed the other side must be the gutter or the edge of the street. But we soon learned not to make dangerous assumptions. Walking along, we felt the changes in the sidewalk. There were ridges telling us of changes ahead. Then we had to decide whether we'd have to turn a corner or cross the street.

On this fine morning, we'd be crossing a busy street safely. We guessed it would be where traffic was light, but were we ever in for a surprise.

We are loaded in the van, and, when the driver stopped to let us off, it sounded like we were in the middle of the freeway. We walked up and down the sidewalk, shore-lining with our shades on. This was to be our first major lesson on "listening." Traffic was moving fast and we were told the ultimate test was for us to cross that busy intersection.

We listened to traffic to the right of us racing in both directions. We were walking along with the traffic until we felt the ridges in the sidewalk. Then we were forced to make a decision. Do we turn the corner or retreat to the rear like the cowards we were, or do we cross the street?

The cars were screeching to a stop, so the light must have turned red for them. The cross traffic in front of us was now moving. We could hear the cars turning left first, then cars going in both directions. Were we ready to make the trip yet? No, first we listened carefully. When traffic stopped, the light must be turning green again for the cars parallel to us. Next, we heard the far lane turning left in front of us. They stopped and traffic was now moving straight ahead in both directions.

Time to make our move! With a pencil grip on our canes to guide us, we located a different texture of the sidewalk and the pavement. Then, using the cane out in front revolving ahead of us, we proceeded across the street. We hurried our steps when we heard the cars slowing down because we knew the light must have changed again. Wow! Simple as that. Reversing the method, we returned to the other side, safe and sound.

We realized now why the proper use of the cane was so important. Another reason to use the long white cane was so the drivers would recognize us in their path. Any of the drivers wanting to make a right turn against the light would see our canes and use (we hoped!) more caution.

We were amazed that crossing a street could be so safe and simple by using our canes and our ears. Before our vision loss, we depended entirely on sight when crossing streets. A sense of hearing becomes much more intense when we no longer depend on vision. Thank God for giving us all of these senses.

If this adventure were the only project we had planned for the week, we would have felt it worth our time being away from home. But, this was just the beginning of another action-packed week.

We were informed we would be cooking a buffet lunch on Saturday for about 40 visitors. Our project on computers was to increase recipes meant for six people into enough food for 40 people. Then we made out the shopping list, dividing it among our three different groups. The next day, with our lists in hand, we went to a local grocery store. Using the skills we learned before, and, with help from a store shopper, we did our shopping.

After lunch, some of us had a short class on applying make up. Vain, as we were, we found this helpful. The counselor teaching the class was totally blind. She sold cosmetics at one time and had vast knowledge of different products. She stressed, because we were unaware of how much make up we were applying to our faces, we had a tendency to apply too much. She suggested going to a major store and having clerks help us with different brands and colors.

If you have always worn lots of make up, as Rose had, you may consider having permanent makeup put on your face. This is a process of tattooing the color on. For example, applying eyeliner or using eyebrow pencils was something we found difficult to do with our vision loss. If the makeup was permanently applied, we need not have to worry about going out looking like a clown.

Comments were made about having problems with tooth paste. Our instructor suggested squeezing the paste on our finger or hand and then applying to the toothbrush. Our suggestion was to have our personal tube of toothpaste and apply it directly into our mouths. No mess and no waste. Good idea, huh?

Lois wasn't too excited about the makeup class since she rarely kept her lipstick on after breakfast, but, Rose, well, she has always liked wearing lipstick, even if the color was wrong or she ended up using lip balm thinking it was lipstick. Oh well, we can't all be models or movie stars.

Great things are done by a series of small things brought together.
—Vincent Van Gogh

Chapter 14: Our Story Continues

Now on to the adventures we will never forget! One day, we headed out to a pumpkin patch. With our shades on, we roamed around running into each other until we found just the right pumpkin or gourd to take home. It's surprising what choices we made.

We didn't have the time to get to the corn maze before it closed. So sad! But it just so happened they had a hay maze set up, and we just couldn't resist going through it. The bales of hay were stacked high so nobody could see each other, but that didn't matter anyhow. We had shades on, so tripping on each other and stumbling into bales of hay was some of the excitement.

We eventually found the exit. But wait, where was Rose? We lost her, but we could hear her cries for help. We finally found her fighting her way out of a corner. Even with all that heat, she made our day. We don't have to tell you that being blind isn't bad after all. It was a fun experience and tested our skills.

On the way home we stopped at a Sonic drive-in for

dinner. With shades on, we had a new experience using a reader to order our dinner. A reader was just that. We walked up to the window and they said, "May I help you?" Then we asked them to read the menu. We listened to the selection and ordered whatever sounded good. If we had questions as to what came with a particular item, they explained it to us. It was very much like a drive-up window at a fast food restaurant. Another first experience for us.

It was Wednesday already. We got up early, fixed our own bag lunches, loaded in the van, and were off for the day. The first stop was the ATM machine at a Wells Fargo bank. For the first time we experienced doing our deposits and withdrawals by use of earphones. You guessed it—we had our shades on.

Next, we found out why we had packed our lunches. Our destination was the Amtrak station. We toured the station first, then with shades on we found the clerk at the counter. Asking directions and where to catch the train that will take us to Davis, we shore-lined our way through the tunnel. Boarding the right train, after again asking directions, we were on our way. We stopped at the rose garden area to eat our lunches.

Davis was a unique and interesting town. We stopped at a theater and entered to find our seats, wearing shades again. Time was limited so we didn't stay to watch the movie.

Our journey continued to a farmer's market to complete our mission of buying fresh fruits and vegetables. With shades on and using the pencil grip on our canes, we're happy to say we didn't trip anybody. Everyone was so helpful when we asked questions and didn't get annoyed with us. The bus met us there to take us home. What a day!

The day wasn't over yet, so, using our cooking skills, we prepared vegetables for a huge stir-fry we were having for dinner. We had a large wok cooking outside so we all had our hands into stirring, serving and eating it. We used a large wooden paddle to stir, even though Lois wanted to use her hands.

A blind mentor who had been through this program many years before told us of his experiences. This same training program had changed his life around, both physically and mentally. He spoke intelligently, with wisdom, and gave us many words of encouragement.

Our week was going by just too fast. Up early again the next day and packing lunches, we were on the road at eight twenty five a.m. First thing on our agenda was a stop at the Sacramento International Airport. This was indeed a welcome experience since many of us were hesitant to fly without assistance. With our shades on and using our friendly canes, we followed voices and other sounds to locate the counter. We had so many offers of help, but politely declined, as we explained we were testing our skills. Due to security reasons only a few of us were allowed through the gate. Had we known about it, we could have made earlier arrangements for clearance for all of us.

We took advantage of the experience anyway, used our skills to go up and down the escalator, located the elevator by sound and sniffed our way to the Starbucks' counter. We asked directions to bathrooms and then found our own way to the baggage area by following sounds. Once again we counted our blessings for being able to hear. We shed the shades and, even though we didn't get to practice going through the gate, we were confident we could fly without assistance.

On to Apple Hill where we ate our lunches. Apple Hill was a collective of fruit orchards in the foothills, about 45 minutes from Sacramento, where many enterprising farmers sold apples, pears, nuts, pies, candy, and other goodies, as well as hand-made arts and crafts. We got to roam around and visited all the booths before we chose our own shade moments. Many of us remembered going to Apple Hill in prior years when it was only a wide place in the road. We were amazed at how much it had changed. Our souvenirs consisted mainly of apple pies, donuts and lots of chocolates. Our group pictures and video were taken in the chocolate area. No surprise there.

Were we just getting old or was everyone as exhausted as we were? Each of us fixed our own hamburgers for dinner and ate once again with shades attached. You would have thought by now they would be permanently attached or worn out.

Our nightly fireside discussions were so touching. Listening to how each person was affected by our experiences, all the time watching each one grow, was so gratifying.

Friday was not only a day of cooking and preparing for all the Saturday visitors, but we had a couple more adventures to have to round out our week.

We went to a public bus stop. Again with shades on, we asked the bus driver if he was bus number 88, because we wanted to go downtown. We paid our fare, told him we were going to Macy's, and asked if he would let us know when we were at our destination.

Once we found our way into Macy's and were then allowed to do some window shopping without our shades. With the help of their courteous clerks, we tried a few cosmetics.

The van took us home, and it was time to get ready for our last adventure. We were taken to a fancy Italian restaurant for dinner. We sat at a large round table, and food was served family style. Since we ate without our shades on, it was a very rewarding treat.

Graduation day and the brunch went well. How did we ever survive the week? We couldn't begin to put a price on the value of all the training and education we just completed. We can't possibly thank the Society for the Blind enough for giving us this opportunity. Everything was so well planned and practical. We now had our chance to go home and live very productive lives.

We said our good-byes to all the staff and new friends, knowing full well we would be seeing all of them again. We were eager to go home and share our enthusiasm with everyone. The retreat house, however, will always be our home away from home.

There are two ways to meeting difficulties. You alter the difficulties or you alter yourself to meet them.
—Phyllis Bottome

Chapter 15: Additional Training

Don't go away, this isn't the end of our story yet. Now that we came home from the advanced retreat with unbridled enthusiasm, we were more determined than ever to get the word out to the whole world. We had a vital message to deliver, but how were we going to accomplish this?

We could offer people the chance to attend a support group meeting, but we couldn't force anyone to go. There are always so many excuses and many of these are legitimate. Underneath many of these excuses is fear and resistance by not willing to accept the fact they are going blind.

We too remember how we slithered into the back row when we attended our first support group meeting. Who would ever believe there are so many individuals with vision loss? Some are so much worse off than we are, others may not be as bad. When people first learn they have macular degeneration, they are often in complete denial. After giving it more thought, they somehow admit they must be prepared for what lies ahead. This is the first step forward—at least it was for us. We were determined to be independent and able to enjoy our lives when we could no longer depend on our vision.

We were stymied trying to find a way to solve this urge we had to tell the world about how our lives had been transformed. Actually it was much more than an urge. It was more like an itch we couldn't scratch.

Maybe, we thought, *we could stand on the street corner with a billboard attached, handing out brochures.* We refused this antic, so this not-so-brilliant idea was nixed from the start.

One day, during some deep thought, a light turned on upstairs. "We'll write a book!" Rose exclaimed. We were already attending writing classes. Lois was writing her memoirs while Rose was writing a romance novel and just finishing a mystery book.

We put all of these projects on the back burner and seriously concentrated on a book about our experiences with macular degeneration. Writing that first page was the most difficult. After starting at least a dozen times, we soon recognized our weaknesses. But we received much encouragement from our writing group, keeping us in focus. We were determined to get this message out to you. This was the birth of the book you are reading now.

Rose can't read or see to type any more so she is taking advantage of the computer classes offered through the Society for the Blind. These classes are offered free of charge to anyone who qualifies, and transportation is also furnished. To qualify one has to be legally blind.

Lois has a bigger hang-up because she didn't know the first thing about how to type or operate a computer. Oh, she knows how to play solitaire and poker on it, but that was all. This puzzled the writing group. "Who doesn't know how to type these days?" they said. Lois reminded them it had been 65 years since she had typed in school.

By sheer embarrassment and mounds of determination, not to mention help from her family, Lois learned to send e-mails and use the word processor. Even though it is a one-finger process, she feels it's still quite an accomplishment.

As you can see, the intensive retreat has opened many doors for us. We were both offered a mentor training class. Rose was busy with her computer class, but Lois attended it. All of the members taking the mentor training had already been through the intensive training. This class was not only a refresher course for all of us, but we received training on how to help others to learn new skills. It was difficult instructing others how to learn, without resisting the urge to do much of the work for them.

Our first training day was on the all- important cane travel. With our canes and shades on, we had to explain the importance and use of the cane to our mentors. To confuse us they asked us many foolish questions and, of course, we gave them many foolish answers. The emphasis on cane travel was actually the basis for all the training.

The training consisted of four different sessions, each class followed by in-depth discussions with our counselors. One session on household survival covered a lot of territory. Another was on the importance of Braille, and all of its many benefits when we no longer can see. Braille is a real challenge, but two of the members who were taking special classes said if we only worked on three letters at a time it would be much easier.

As we've mentioned before, there are Braille schools available offering instruction over the phone. Many of these classes are free of charge. For more information on available schools in your area, contact the Society for the Blind. The Hadley School for the Blind is one source with on-line registration.

Our last day, graduation day, was spent at the mall at the shopping center. It was our last chance to help our mentors with shades on with how to find their way when they are shopping. There were a lot of curious bystanders with various questions, which we gladly answered. Our students found out it's not so bad being blind, because they could "see" so much more by using their other senses. They learned to ask questions and found places by themselves. We hoped we were showing the public we were not invalids but very capable of living a normal life.

We found our way to a nearby pizza restaurant where we had all the food we could possibly eat, without our shades. Here, we proudly accepted our diplomas.

As we progressed with our individual projects, we continued to write new chapters to our book. We had absolutely no time to feel sorry for ourselves. We were both very busy bringing new ideas and speakers to our low vision support group.

So you see, we were on a mission. We threw away all of our crutches. We assumed control of our own lives, knowing there'd be an occasional bump or two in the road, but nothing that a little laughter wouldn't solve. We believed, after every storm, the sun would shine again, so rise and shine and follow us on our journey.

Peace of mind is that mental condition in which you have accepted the worst.
—Lin Yutang

Chapter 16: Rose's Confession—School Daze

My first scheduled day for instruction at the Society for the Blind was so exciting. My appointment was for an evaluation in mobility and independent living. The person who was to pick me up had another obligation and was late. Very late. When I got to the school, I felt excited all over again. There were lots of people of all ages there, conversing and mingling. It appeared everyone was happy.

I couldn't wait until it was my turn. I talked to my first instructor for about an hour and a half. I wanted to talk longer, but I was informed the session was for an evaluation only.

At noon everyone had lunch. I brought my peanut butter and jelly sandwich. (Isn't that what most children bring to school on their first day?)

My second class was after one o'clock. Then I waited and ended up talking to another teacher for another hour and a half. I wanted to learn; I was ready. But it did not happen on my first day of school.

On the way home, there were three of us being driven to Roseville. I am an out-going friendly person, and after many miles of silence, I finally decided to break the ice.

After we introduced ourselves, I asked the young woman sitting next to me, "Do you have macular degeneration also?"

She was quiet for a few minutes, and then she shouted, "No, I'm blind."

I felt so badly. I could have bitten off my tongue.

Mile after mile of silence – *again I tried*. "Isn't this a beautiful day?"

Once more, I could have died right there. What was I thinking? She just finished telling me she was blind, and now here I was asking if she could see this beautiful day.

Wow, that was a very long ride back to Roseville. I learned something, though—to keep my mouth shut until the other person speaks. This was not the first time I said an inappropriate thing, and possibly not the last, but I will tell you I listen now to my little voice before I let the big voice come out of my mouth.

I survived my first day of school and looked forward to my second. This time, the driver was on time when he picked me up, and we dashed off to the Society for the Blind.

Nervousness is something we all try to hide. When I saw the coffee pot, I decided to pour myself a full cup to calm my nerves. After thinking about it, for a minute, though, I realized everything that goes in must come out. I settled for only one-third cup.

I met the Mobility instructor I had the previous week. Eager to start my lesson, I put my cup of coffee on the desk and proceeded to take off my coat. The instructor went to get something off her desk, and what do you think happened? She hit the cup and coffee spilled over part of the desk on which sat a white cuddly bear.

"Oh, my gosh, I'm so sorry," I said. I started pulling out tissues from an open box and began cleaning the mess up. The coffee ran into her white bear, which now had a brown bottom.

I mopped up the desk while she took Mr. Bear into the bathroom to clean him up. I could tell by the way she held it, she had special feelings for that bear.

The first rule we learned at the retreat in our cooking class was: Never put a cup of anything on the counter. My little coffee spill proved our instructor was right again.

Most of the time, our positive attitude and determination keeps, Lois and I on the right tract. However, there were times when we, too, fell on our knees and questioned, "Why me?"

I was fortunate to receive computer instructions by a teacher from the Society For the Blind. Having the van pick me up and return me home after the lesson was completed made it so easy for me to attend the classes.

We mentioned before about some of the computer programs in the market today to help meet the challenges of those of us who are experiencing vision loss. One of my favorites is Dragon Naturally Speaking, which types the words we speak into a microphone plugged into the computer. The Society usually recommends this program to students who have limited use of their hands or arms. Incidentally, Lois uses this one mainly because she doesn't type too well.

Zoom Text is another very powerful magnifying program, which speaks as you type, or will read the typed material to you after you have typed it. This is one of my favorite programs, but you need some vision to be proficient at it.

Then there's the program, Jaws. It's the program the Society recommends, since no vision is needed to use it efficiently. Since it works by keyboard commands, you will need to memorize many of the keys, which you will use over and over again.

These are just a few of the many programs on the market today.

I still have a little vision, so I was emphatic about using Zoom Text. I had to use very large magnified fonts and occasionally use my magnifying glass to find the keys I needed. I was still using my eyesight, and it was a great program, which made me feel good. Are you aware what happens to a computer screen when you enlarge the fonts? Right, it covers a page with letters, but few sentences. My first teacher kept telling me Zoom Text was not for me. Even I would admit I couldn't read the letters on the screen.

"Then you need to learn Jaws," he would say to me. He had me almost convinced this is where I should be in my computer instructions, but then he accepted another position, and I was placed with a new teacher.

It was *déjà vu* all over again. "I want Zoom Text," I'd say. "When I can no longer read it, I'll go to Jaws."

My new instructor began trying to tell me in a nice way Zoom Text was too difficult for me to work with. But being stubborn, as most of us are, I'd say, "Enlarge the font one size larger."

She could see I was struggling with this decision. I felt like a pig headed for the slaughterhouse. No one was saying this, nor were they applying this type pressure. This is what I was doing to myself by not facing facts, nor being honest with myself.

"I'll start using Jaws when I need it."

Finally my teacher had enough. She contacted my social worker and spoke about my reluctance to start this program.

The social worker called me and spoke very kindly and wisely, explaining why I was having a difficult time admitting to myself, I could no longer use my vision to see, as I did in the past. I was not totally blind. I could still see. But I was legally totally blind and could no longer read small print. It was simply too difficult to admit to myself that I'd eventually become totally blind. Nor did I want to admit it to my teacher or my counselor.

The big break-through came when I, at long last, admitted it to myself.

"I can no longer use Zoom Text," I told my instructor. "I need to go to the program, which does not need sight to function efficiently. I need Jaws."

As I write this, the tears are gathering in my eyes. I feel them flowing down my cheeks and into my mouth. I can taste the salty moisture. You, too, may be in this same situation where your heart is breaking. I shared this with you so you will know you are not alone and it's not the end of the world, but just another bump in the road to get over. I realized, in the long run, using Jaws would make it easier to accomplish my goal, which was the completion of this book. So there was a silver lining in my dark cloud after all.

I hope my little confession about the computer will help you take another step forward to face the rays of hope that are there for us every day.

I cannot tell you often enough, what a difference the Society for the Blind, their retreats, and everyone who spent so many hours helping me, have changed my life. When I was sighted, I was a successful professional. I was very sure of myself most all the time. At a minute's notice, I would jump into my car and take my family and friends who needed help to any place they wanted. I was always available for anyone who needed a helping hand.

As I lost my vision, I found myself staying away from everyone, for fear they would ask me to help them do or to go some place, like the store, shopping, and movies.

My usual happy-go-lucky attitude changed. I found myself withdrawing more and more within myself. Then the day came when I had to tell the world I no longer could drive or work at my profession.

I started writing novels because that was something I could do without anyone around. But I noticed it was getting more difficult to write, edit, and operate the computer as I had for many years.

I am now doing fairly well with the program Jaws on the computer. I have finally allowed my brain to grow.

You've heard the term *open-minded.* Well, I am open to almost everything. My teacher taught me how to use Kurzweil, a program that can actually read to me. Now I can read books like I did before—well, maybe not as quickly as I once did, not yet anyway.

When I write and need to edit my work, I use Jaws, the computer program, to help me be more efficient in my writing. I am not saying I have it all down pat, because this has been a challenging program for me to learn. But, there is not much I can't do today that I used to do, and I must agree Jaws is far simpler to use than getting my magnifying glass up to the computer screen all the time. The program reads the typed material back to me, and my speed is getting better all the time. I am only sorry I was so head strong and vain, wanting to do it my way, because I could have been even further ahead in my productivity.

My friends keep telling me, "We can't tell you can't see."

And I answer, "I see with my fingers, cane and nose."

They laugh.

It feels so good to be independent. No, I am not driving, like Lois, and I must agree her sight is much better than mine. But I have come to accept all the bumps I've had to go over and giving up driving has been one of them. I'm sure there are still many to conquer, but I'm determined I can do it.

I'd like to tell you what my long-range goals and plans are, but I've been hesitant to do so because I thought maybe I was only "wishing on a star." But it turned out wishes can come true.

I mentioned I was a real estate broker. In the field of real estate, it is mandatory for agents/brokers to complete a minimum of forty-five hours of continuous education to renew our license every four years. My license expired in 2005. Unable to read, I figured I could not complete this feat, so my license expired. Another loss to get over.

You can imagine my joy when I checked the mail under my Closed Circuit TV (CCTV) and found a post card from a real estate exam school. It advertised an open book final exam when completing the forty-five hour instructions.

I sent for the material and had my daughter read the material to me. She asked the questions, and I answered them and then she put the "X" in the box.

I was elated, excited, and proud when I found out I had passed the exam. In order to receive my license, I had to send a monetary fee to the Real Estate Department Licensing Board which would then send me my license.

Each day I go to the mailbox to look for the license, which is now forthcoming. Yes, I am very proud of myself. You, too, can reach your goals, whatever they may be.

Remember as kids, how we built fantastic homes a block at a time or sand castles in the sand, a handful at a time?

Remember, as well, you cannot only reach for the stars, but for the entire universe.

Twenty years from now you will be more disappointed by the things you didn't do than by the ones you did. So throw off the bowlines. Sail away from the safe harbor. Catch the trade winds in your sails. Explore. Dream. Discover.
—Mark Twain

Chapter 17: Lois's Update

My life has been anything but boring. Having a big supportive family has helped to fill in the gaps that may have collected negative thoughts and self-pity.

Losing my vision has been a challenge. I appreciate each day and really never worry about tomorrow. Since I am already way beyond 70 years of age, my family tells me I am living on borrowed time. I would love to borrow another 15 or 20 years, so I can complete some of my unfinished projects.

In my garage, I have at least ten large containers full of craft projects—some for different holidays and some hanging around since my Girl Scout days. Do I plan on ever finishing them? Oh yes. Along beside them in three more bins are three quilt tops ready to be tied. I started a cookbook for zucchini recipes when zucchini was discovered to be great for cakes, cookies, and bread. I also started a family cookbook, which I plan to leave as a legacy for all of my grandchildren. Just in case I run out of things to do, I have begun writing a book on my memoirs. I just don't ever want to run out of things to do.

I belong to an active macular degeneration support group, which I am spearheading. We organized almost two years ago with seven members attending the first meeting. Now we have about 65 on the roster. Of course, they don't all attend every meeting, but we do send out notices each month with the agenda. Rose cleverly finds topics of interest for each meeting. Two days before each meeting, we follow through with members that help us make reminder calls to everyone to attend the meetings. This has been so helpful and rewarding, so that forgetting is no excuse for not attending.

I have continued with all of the advanced training available, and, therefore, made many new friends. I am available to help as a mentor or in the outreach program, whenever needed. Life continues to be rewarding and beyond all dreams.

I do have a confession to make, however, as I haven't exactly been as honest as I should be. After all the training and positive reinforcement in using our other skills, I had one big hang up. I couldn't admit to myself I couldn't drive anymore. I kept the keys to my car in my pocket, just in case I needed them. You might say I had a key hang-up.

I even told my ophthalmologist I was no longer driving, so he wouldn't report me to the Department of Motor Vehicles. After all, my license was still good until 2008. I could still see the red and green signals, even though I couldn't read road signs. When the sun was shining brightly, though, I was blinded. When it rained, I couldn't see the lines on the road. At night all I saw was the two dots from oncoming cars. But, I never had an accident or even a traffic citation, so I felt I must have been a good, safe driver.

Driving home from my other daughter's house one day, I was following a big semi truck on the freeway. I decided to pass him, but, as I glanced in the rearview mirror, I couldn't see a thing. The sun blinded me when I looked out the side windows. Fortunately, I had enough sense to slow down and follow the sign posted on the rear of the truck.

I felt the presence of someone riding with me as I drove home on a wing and a prayer. As I neared home, I only had one more corner to turn. It was a left turn signal, and, as I turned I ran over the middle divider with my rear tire. I drove into my garage in tears.

I told my daughter, "Don't ever let me drive again. That curb might have been a child I couldn't see." Sadly, I hung my car keys on a hook where I could occasionally glance at them as I walked by.

One day our support group invited a speaker from the transportation department to attend one of our meetings. He came in a dial-a-ride bus and brought us much needed information showing us how easy it is to travel by bus. It's great and, with the extra help from my daughter, I am adapting well, using an alternative system for getting out and about.

As time went on my vision was becoming more blurred and colors were reduced to just black and white. I was so devastated when I could no longer read the sports page with my magnifier, I decided it was time to see the specialist again.

That turned out to be a good decision because he scheduled me for cataract surgery. Knowing all the risks of either seeing again or losing the vision altogether, I chose to take the chance. It was a piece of cake. When he took the patch off the first eye after the surgery, the whole world came alive again. Grass and trees were a vivid green and the sky so blue, I couldn't believe it. I really had been living in a fog. Please note, this procedure won't always work for everyone, but I'm so grateful it helped me.

The best news came when I returned to see the specialist. My vision had improved so much, he said I would be able to take the driver's test and get my license back. Thank heaven, I still had my license for two more years.

I remembered to check the Amsler grid posted on my mirror each day to make sure the lines don't suddenly disappear in a blur. It is something we must be aware could happen at any given time.

I was free again to put the car keys back into my pocket and do some of my own driving. What a thrill to have that wonderful feeling of independence again. Suddenly, I remembered the panic I felt before. To prevent this from happening again, I limited my driving to familiar areas without much traffic.

I moved my recliner back away from the television so I could watch TV with the rest of the family. I read the sports page in the paper again. Life was great.

During this interlude in my life, I did accomplish one goal. I could no longer read my own writing, so I was determined to learn how to operate the computer. You can't begin to count the mistakes I made while learning. I'm certain that little guy who is hiding behind the screen was about to blow a gasket. I am typing now, still with one finger, working on several writing projects.

I can now keep in touch with my family. I always wondered if any of them ever learned to write by hand because they were all raised on the computer. Now they can run, but they can't hide. I send them short messages along with all the jokes. This will, nine times out of ten, bring a response via e-mail. Just to receive, "Love you, Grandma" makes my heart jump with joy.

My goals at the present time are all wrapped up in one project. Rose and I are determined to publish this book with our experiences and words of encouragement so that we can get the word out to all of you. Life can be wonderful. Laughter is healing. Believe us when we tell you, a little laughter does go a long, long way.

How far you go in life depends on your being tender with the young, compassionate with the aged, sympathetic with the striving, tolerant of the weak and strong. Because sometime in your life, you will have been all of those.
—George Washington Carver

Chapter 18: Finale, But Not the End

We have been reminiscing about the changes in our lives since that first day at the Society for the Blind. What a blessing that intensive training retreat was on our lives. We were like two lost and scared little puppies, wondering what on earth we were doing there.

Thanks to the training we received from the Society for the Blind, we found our new way in life. We take life one day at a time, one step at a time. It's been one heck of a year, and we are excited about life's possibilities. Who knows? Maybe we could even teach a wildcat to play the banjo!

Our reactions used to vary when we met someone with a disability, whether they were in a wheelchair or walking with a long white cane. Do we move out of the way for them, turn our heads so we don't face them, or feel our hearts going out to them with deep sympathy. No, we now meet them with a smile on our faces and a mutual understanding of the extra effort they have put forth to live a normal life. Each has adapted a different lifestyle, taking advantage of all the opportunities available to keep them going in the mainstream of society.

We all want to be responsible for our own destiny. It begins by opening that door and stepping out into the world with our heads held high. *Why don't we go shopping today? We know how to ride a bus. Outside of driving a car, what is there we can't do? We know how to cook, clean house, do the laundry, and care for our families.*

So many times friends or family try to help us too much. They need to ask first if we might need the help. The thoughtfulness is greatly appreciated, but we feel so much more confident when we accomplish things ourselves.

The communities are opening so many opportunities for us. Obstacles in walking have been removed, so we can now cross streets and enter buildings. Employers are accepting people with disabilities as individuals capable of the same needs and feelings as themselves. They now will hire disabled persons based on their qualifications for the job.

We have all met people in our lives that have absolutely amazed us with their accomplishments. Lois observed one such person:

"I delivered mail earlier in my career, and I watched a totally blind man paint the outside of his two-story home. He would climb up and down his ladder with ease. He placed his left hand away from the strip he had already painted, then proceeded to paint until he touched his hand. He then moved the ladder over. It took him several weeks to complete the house, but what a thrill that must have been for him. I didn't climb the ladder to inspect his work, but it certainly looked great from the sidewalk."

Now we don't mean you have to go out and paint your house. Just ask yourself, "What goal could I set for myself?" Then get busy and do it. If you stumble on that bump in the road we have often talked about, just remember help can be on its way if you ask.

We both love what we are doing. It is such a rewarding feeling when we have reached out and helped just one person. Of course, our goals are set high hoping to reach everyone with vision problems.

We might suggest enacting a "Celebrate the Handicapped Day," one in which everyone can be involved. It would be great if the disabled, blind, deaf, or otherwise could spend one day in school each year. We could describe to all, young and old, our challenges in daily life. We laugh, we cry, we get angry, we plan and dream just the same as they do. Students would have a better understanding and no longer be afraid or cynical of those who have been incapacitated in some way. Maybe they would understand how human we really are. Wouldn't this be a great goal we could all strive for?

As Rose and Lois both say, "Let's get the lead out and move on with the rest of our lives. Good luck, and let us enjoy the rest of our days."

We leave you now with a quote from George Bernard Shaw that best sums up our message of hope:

This is the true meaning of life: to live for something recognized by yourself to be a mighty cause; to be a force of nature rather than a feverish clod of grievances and ailments, complaining that the universe is not devoting itself to make you happy. Life is its own splendid justification. I want to be used up when I die; the harder I work, the more that I live. I don't believe that life is a flickering candle. I believe it is a splendid torch. I want to make it burn as brightly as I can before I hand it on to my children.

EPILOGUE

We looked up the definition of "epilogue," thinking we would discover a unique reason for including an epilogue, but decided to use the simplest, easiest definition: "A short speech."

After the final retreat, we remained connected to the Society for the Blind. With the holiday season just around the corner, we attended their Christmas party, which was held not only to celebrate the holidays, but also to give everyone who attended and completed the retreat a chance to share their experiences.

There were many different ethnicities represented that evening, and the strangest thing happened. No matter how they spoke or what language they used, we all said the same thing. We thanked the Society for the opportunity they offered us. We all had a great time, and agreed we did not need vision to have a good time with friends.

If I gave you a crisp twenty-dollar bill and asked, if you wanted it, would you say, "Yes"?

Say I took that twenty-dollar bill and threw it in the dirt, then stomped on it and asked, "Who will take this twenty dollar bill?" You would say, "I want it."

If I took the twenty dollar bill, stomped on it, kicked it, crumbled it, you would still want it. Why?

Because it still had the same value as the crisp new twenty-dollar bill I showed you.

Like the twenty-dollar bill, we still have the same value. No matter if we have macular degeneration. No, we are not crisp, new twenty-dollar bills, but we have the same value as others who can see perfectly.

Lois has continued being a mentor at all retreats and is very active in the Outreach program. She can speak from her vast experience and delights the audience with her humor.

Rose continues her computer class, still trying to conquer Jaws. She said they named the program correctly because, if you don't watch out, it will eat you alive.

She has received her Brokers Real Estate License and is now helping her niece with several real estate transactions.

So, dear friends, we want you to think of us whenever you come to a bump in the road and want to give up—don't. Reach out and bring the rewards back with you. And when you achieve your goal, send us a note and share it with us. We'd love to hear from you.

Rose Gasser and Lois Brooks

Rose Gasser's Biography

I was born in Martinez, California, to immigrant parents from Spain. My dad was a farmer and my mother a cannery worker. I have nine brothers and sisters—two boys, the first-born and the last, and seven girls in between. I happen to be the seventh and youngest girl, a fact I have always felt was special.

I went to Castro Valley Grammar School and attended Hayward High School, until 1945 when my parents decided to move to Loomis, California, and became fruit and chicken ranchers. This did not make me happy at all. I was a city gal, not a country bumpkin.

I graduated from Placer Union High School in Auburn and started working the day after graduation as the office manager for a fruit packing company.

I married and had two wonderful children. My son has three sons and one daughter. My daughter has a very large four-legged family, whose members consist of a three-pound Chihuahua, an adorable apricot poodle, a donkey, and a large, beautiful, black Friesian horse.

I've been a secretary, bookkeeper, and office administrator. The last twenty-nine years I spent in real estate, until macular degeneration crossed my path and literally got me in the eyes. With this onset I had to close the old doors that had opened for me. However, I am very busy now opening all the new, shiny, larger doors to a world of endless possibilities.

Lois Brooks' Biography

I was born and grew up on a farm in the Midwest. My parents worked hard trying to make a living for my brother, two sisters, and myself during the depression years. We were poor but didn't realize it since we always had food on the table.

After a bad marriage and three little ones to feed, I moved to California. There I remarried and inherited three more children.

My husband worked in construction so we moved around, each time creating a new experience, a new challenge, and many good memories of the family.

I have been retired for twenty years now and keep busy trying to remember the birthdays of my 31 grandchildren and great grandchildren.

After retiring, I started writing my memoirs for my family, only to have it interrupted with macular degeneration. But I view it as only another challenge, and since I don't intend to stop living, I have set another goal—to get this book out to everyone.

RESOURCES

SOCIETY FOR THE BLIND: 916-452-8271

AMERICAN COUNCIL OF THE BLIND:
1-800-424-8666

AMERICAN COUNCIL OF THE BLIND CALIFORNIA STATE
AFFILIATE: 1-800-221-6369

BRAILLE AND TALKING BOOK LIBRARY:
1-800-952-5666

BRAILLE INSTITUTE OF AMERICA: 323-663-1111

HADLEY SCHOOL FOR THE BLIND: 1-800-323-4238

CALIFORNIA ACCESS NEWS: 1-800-665-4667

CALIFORNIA DEPARTMENT OF REHABILITATION: 916-322-8500

CALIFORNIA TELEPHONE ACCESS PROGRAM: 1-800-806-1191

CALIFORNIA RELAY SERVICE: 1-800-735-2922

EYE DOG FOUNDATION: 1-860-243-5200

GUIDE DOGS FOR THE BLIND: 1-800-295-4050

PLACER COUNTY VISUAL SERVICE CENTER:
530-885-1154

LION'S CENTER FOR THE BLIND: 510-450-4016

SACRAMENTO REGIONAL TRANSIT: 916-321-2877

SACRAMENTO SUPPORT GROUP: 916-452-8271

SOCIAL SECURITY ADMINISTRATION:
1-800-772-1213

Amsler Grid

- Post the Amsler grid in an easy to-see-place.
- Stand about a foot away.
- Wearing your glasses, cover or close one eye and focus on the black dot in the center.
- Note any vision changes such as black spots or wavy lines.
- Repeat the above steps with the other eye.
- Call your doctor promptly if you notice any changes.

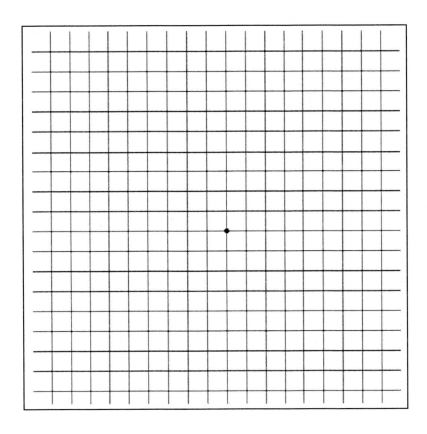

ISBN 1425113648

9 781425 113643